FISHBOURNE

A DAY IN A
ROMAN
Palace

T. D. Triggs

WAYLAND

Titles in the Series

Fishbourne – A Day in a Roman Palace
Barley Hall – A Day in a Medieval Town House

Series Editor: Cathy Baxter
Book Designer: Jean Wheeler
Artist: Chris Forsey
Consultant: David Rudkin

First Published in 1997 by Wayland (Publishers) Ltd
61 Western Road, Hove, East Sussex, BN3 1JD, England

British Library Cataloging in Publication Data
Triggs, Tony D.
Fishbourne: A Day in a Roman Palace
(What Life Was Like Series)
I. Title II. Series
936.226204

HARDBACK ISBN 0 7502 1609 3

Typeset by Jean Wheeler, England.
Colour reproduction by Page Turn, Hove, E. Sussex
Printed and bound in Italy by G. Canale &
CSpA, Turin

Picture acknowledgements:
Arbeia Roman Fort and Museum 31;
Dixon 3, 4, 8, 11 (bottom left and
right), 13 (top and bottom), 17
(bottom), 18, 19, 22, 23, 25, 26, 27
(bottom), 29; English Heritage 30
(bottom); Francesca Motisi 6, 7, 9, 21,
27; Fishbourne Roman Palace 12, 14,
15 (top and bottom). National
Museums and Galleries of Wales 30;
N. Cooke author photograph; Roman
Army Museum 30; St Albans Museum
11 (top), 14 (inset).

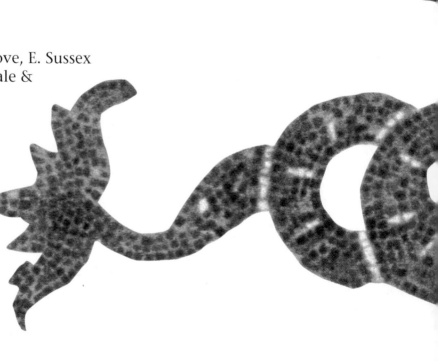

Contents

Introduction

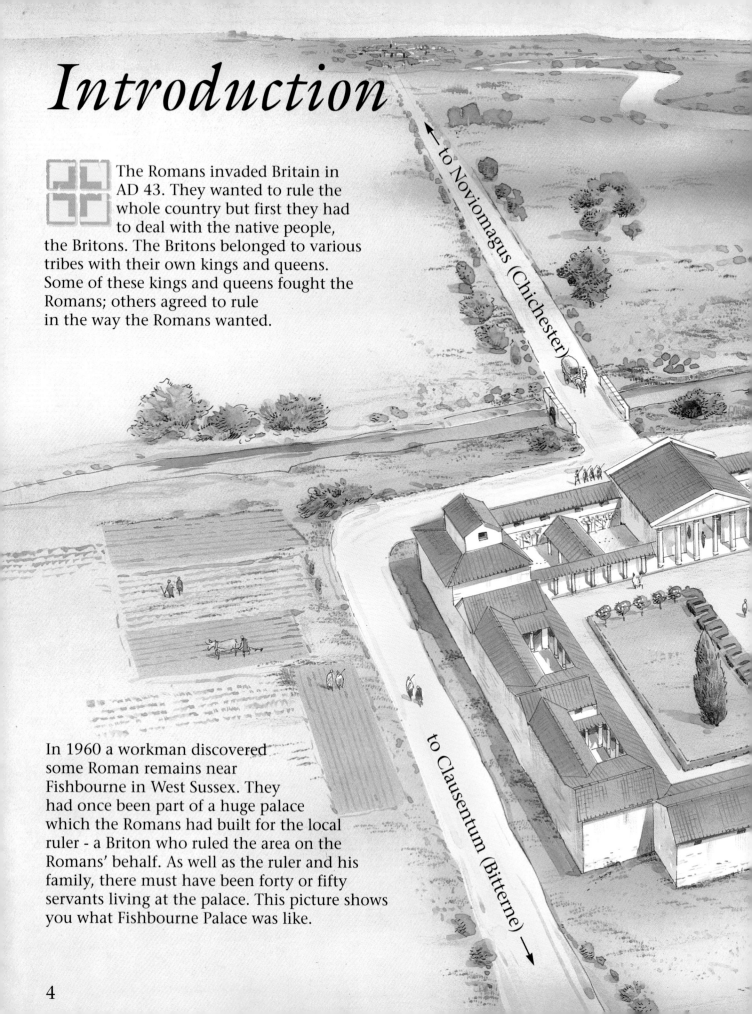

The Romans invaded Britain in AD 43. They wanted to rule the whole country but first they had to deal with the native people, the Britons. The Britons belonged to various tribes with their own kings and queens. Some of these kings and queens fought the Romans; others agreed to rule in the way the Romans wanted.

to Noviomagus (Chichester)

to Clausentum (Bitterne)

In 1960 a workman discovered some Roman remains near Fishbourne in West Sussex. They had once been part of a huge palace which the Romans had built for the local ruler - a Briton who ruled the area on the Romans' behalf. As well as the ruler and his family, there must have been forty or fifty servants living at the palace. This picture shows you what Fishbourne Palace was like.

N

After the remains were discovered, archaeologists quickly set to work. They began to uncover more and more of the site.

After eight years' work, the archaeologists had traced the shape of over forty rooms, and they had still studied only half the palace. The buildings had been arranged in a square around a garden the size of a football pitch. The Roman builders (or their British slaves) had laid the garden out with lawns, ornamental hedges and paths.

▲ The walls of the palace had disappeared but it is easy to see where they had stood. Can you see the position of the walls in this photograph of the museum as it is today?

Today, half the garden and buildings have been destroyed or hidden by a busy road and modern houses. Most of the archaeologists' work has been done in the northern half of the site, which had not been damaged nearly as much.

The remains along the northern edge of the garden have been studied in detail and covered with a modern building to protect them from the weather. Visitors can enter this building and the northern half of the garden and see the Roman remains for themselves.

▼ One of the rooms has a grave dug into the floor and visitors can see a skeleton lying in it. No one knows why the body was buried here, but archaeologists think it happened after a fire had burned the building down.

Many of the floors at Fishbourne Palace were beautifully decorated with mosaics. Mosaics were patterns or pictures made from tiny pieces of coloured stone, pottery or glass.

The craftspeople covered part of the floor in smooth soft mortar and added the coloured pieces before the mortar went hard. They carried on in a similar way until the floor was completely covered.

▲ This is one of the best mosaics at Fishbourne. In its centre, you can see Cupid, the god of love. The mosaic also shows horses and panthers with special tails for swimming!

The Romans based some of their mosaics on their favourite stories, including stories of their gods and heroes. In the mosaic shown on the opposite page, there is a picture of a boy riding on the back of a dolphin. The boy's wings tell us that he is Cupid, the Roman god of love. He is carrying a trident (a three-pronged spear). If he wanted someone to fall in love he could make himself invisible and use his trident to pierce their heart.

Mosaics and other clues in the ground tell us a lot about life at Fishbourne and the things the people thought about. The rest of this book describes a day at the palace. There is plenty happening!

▼ Here is a close-up of the same mosaic. The only ordinary animal in the mosaic is this little bird. Some people think that it is the sign the artist used to show who he was.

Night

It is night-time – and cold – but the ruling family are warm and comfortable in their beds. Outside, one of the servants is working hard to keep the fire of the hypocaust blazing. To a Briton like him it seems strange to have a fire outside the building, against one of the walls. However, the hot air heats the room as it flows along small tunnels under the floor. The glass in the bedroom windows is green, and as dawn breaks the room is filled with coloured light.

As the master gets up, servants arrive with breakfast. They light the oil lamp on the dressing table. The servants then help the master to wash, comb his hair and put on perfume. Finally the master makes his way to the toilet.

◀ A Roman oil lamp found in Britain. It was fuelled with olive oil that came by ship from Italy.

▼ This wall-painting shows a Roman woman pouring perfume into a small vase.

▼ Some Roman toilets were built so that two people could use them at once!

Dawn

 Fishbourne Palace stands near the mouth of a little stream, so boats with cargoes of fish and seafood call at the palace each day.

The fishermen go to sea at night. They say that the moon draws the fish to the surface. As the boats arrive the servants quickly unload them and put the fish somewhere cool. If they let it go bad in the sun the master will not be pleased and they may be punished.

Fact Box

The Romans used wood and stone for their buildings, and wood was also their main form of fuel. Over the years, the servants at Fishbourne Palace probably chopped down all the trees in the neighbourhood.

Cargo ships arrive at the palace throughout the day, bringing wine and other luxuries. Servants unload the ships then fill them with grain from nearby British farms.

Most of the servants are Britons, and they know very well that the Romans are taking British goods without paying for them. The Romans call it tax but the servants regard it as theft – so they hate being made to load the grain into the ships.

▼ The model and the wall-painting below show you what Roman cargo ships looked like.

◀ A model of Fishbourne Palace showing how it may have appeared in Roman times.

The master is expecting an important guest – a centurion with his eighty soldiers. So the paths must be swept to get rid of all the leaves and twigs, and the carefully shaped bushes in the garden have to be trimmed to perfection.

As they work, the servants can hear other servants in the vegetable gardens around the palace. They are digging up parsnips ready for the master's afternoon meal. There are other sounds too: a squawking noise as one of the servants tries to kill a wild duck, and the rumble and squeak of a wheelbarrow on its way to the kitchen.

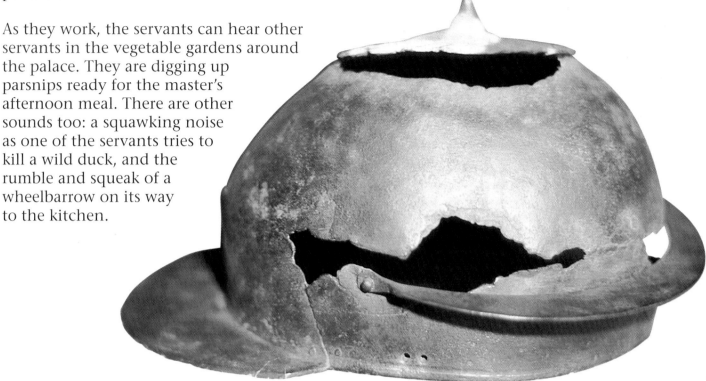

◀ Box hedges in the garden at Fishbourne, planted so they follow the same pattern as the hedges in Roman times.

Inset: A reconstruction of a Roman wooden spade with an original iron spade sheath, found at Fishbourne.

▲ A Roman helmet found in Chichester Harbour.

Suddenly, one of the servants drops his broom and kneels down. He scratches at the roots of the hedge and then leaps up again. There is something gleaming and twinkling between his finger and thumb. 'I've found it!' he cries, 'It's the ring the master's daughter lost!' He rushes into the palace with his precious discovery.

◀ A child's gold ring, found at Fishbourne. It is set with a stone showing a bird.

Mid morning

It is the middle of the morning and the visitors are here. The servants disappear from the garden snatching a few last leaves from the paths as they go.

The centurion leads his party between the pillars of the entrance hall. He is not in his armour today; he is wearing a toga instead. He bows as he reaches the emperor's statue. Beyond it there is a pool with a fountain of sparkling water. One or two of the servants secretly hope that he'll fall right into it!

The guests start to cross the courtyard between the newly trimmed hedges. The servants outside do not see them, and they start to joke and play about. One group of servants is making clay roof tiles.

The last batch of tiles is lying in the sun to dry. The clay is still soft, and one of the servants puts his foot in it. He is wearing his leather shoe, and when he takes it out again it leaves a perfect print in the clay (see below).

Another servant removes his shoe and touches the clay with his bare foot. His workmates tell him to push it right into the clay, but he's frightened that the sores on his foot will show up and give him away.

Fact Box

The palace had about eighty rooms. Some were for servants, but most of the servants probably lived in extra buildings that stood nearby. Over 100 people lived in the palace and the other buildings, so the area must have been like a small town.

▼ A clay roof tile at Fishbourne Palace, with a man's footprint and a shoe print.

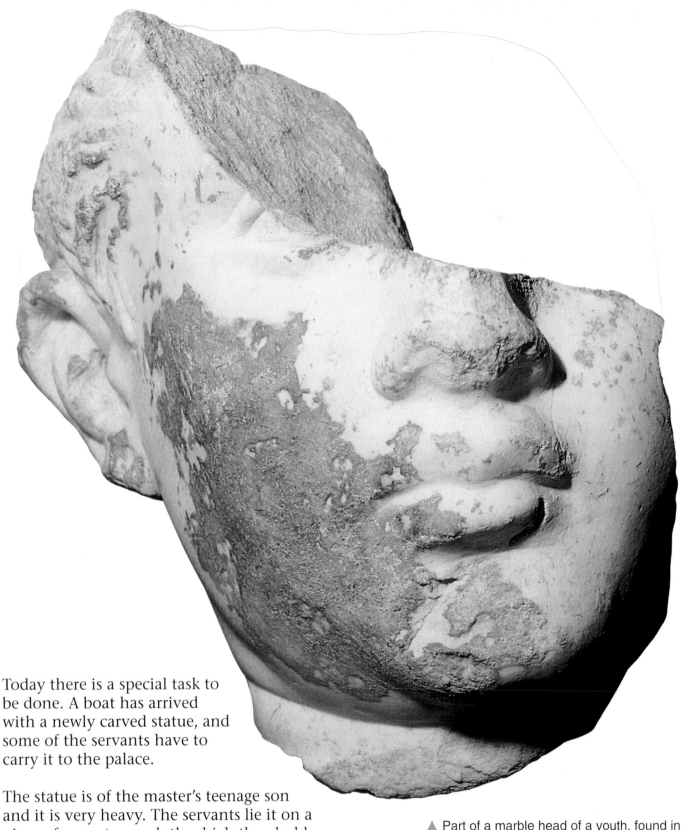

Today there is a special task to
be done. A boat has arrived
with a newly carved statue, and
some of the servants have to
carry it to the palace.

The statue is of the master's teenage son
and it is very heavy. The servants lie it on a
piece of very strong cloth which they hold
by the corners. As well as helping them to
carry it, the cloth protects the statue from
their sweaty hands.

▲ Part of a marble head of a youth, found in
the North Wing of Fishbourne Palace.

There are also statues in the shrine, which is the biggest and grandest room in the palace. Here the walls are lined with statues of gods, not people.

The visitors' horses are restless because a girl from the stables is trying to raise their legs and remove their shoes. Roman horseshoes are made to come off easily, but these horses are tired and hungry after their long journey.

▲ These removable horse shoes are called hippo sandals. Hippos is the Greek word for horse.

Fact Box

Roman horseshoes were made by heating pieces of iron in a hearth until red-hot and then hammering them into shape on an anvil.

Suddenly, one of the horses kicks out, giving the stable girl a nasty bruise on her forehead. The servants are careful to keep the statue well away from the horses' hind (back) legs. What would happen if the statue was kicked? The thought of it lying in pieces makes them very scared.

Midday

A servant is putting new tiles on the roof of the entrance hall. He is perched on the point of the roof like a bird. He is afraid of dropping a tile on to the horses and people below so he is working very carefully.

Looking across the courtyard, he sees the centurion walking towards the audience chamber. He wonders what happens inside. With its marble pillars it seems as important as the entrance hall or the shrine of the gods.

Having repaired the mosaic floor several times, he knows what the audience chamber is like inside. A stone bench curves round the wall at the back. He guesses that the room is the place where important people give speeches.

◄ A view of the audience chamber as it might have looked in Roman times. The walls and roof have been partly removed to show the interior.

▼ This is part of the mosaic floor of a room near to the audience chamber.

The servant's guess is right: the centurion is giving a speech in the Audience Chamber now. He says he wants eighty soldiers to stay at the palace when they march from the south coast to London next week. They'll only be there for a single night but they'll need to be fed. That means killing a dozen sheep and collecting up to 200 eggs.

▲ The girl in this Roman painting is holding two hinged wax writing tablets in one hand and a writing instrument in the other.

The master's scribe notes everything down. He scratches the words on to a wax tablet. Later, the notes will be copied down in pen and ink, and the wax can be smoothed and used again.

The master's children are in the palace schoolroom next to the audience chamber. Like the master's scribe, they are using wax tablets; if they make a mistake they can smooth it out and try again.

▼ A wax tablet was a small wooden board smoothly coated with wax. The palace had beehives where wax and honey could both be collected. The metal writing instrument was called a stylus.

Early afternoon

Servants are busy in the kitchen preparing the meal for the master and his guests. One wall has a row of fireplaces, and flames are licking round joints of meat that are roasting on spits. At every fireplace a sweating servant is adding wood and turning the spit.

▲ A fire is lit on special heat-proof tiles, and then the pan of sauce is placed on a metal stand above the flames.

Other servants are preparing sauces. They grind dried herbs from the palace gardens, then they put them in pans, and mix them up with milk, eggs, honey and spices. They heat and stir each sauce until it is thick and creamy.

Important guests, like the centurion, must have very smooth sauce, so the servants remove any bits of stalk that haven't been properly ground. This means pouring the sauce through strainers before they serve it.

The servants can have any sauce and bits of stalk that get left in the strainers. They chew the stalks and lick up the sauce.

▶ This bronze strainer was used to remove any unground ingredients from the sauce.

Late afternoon

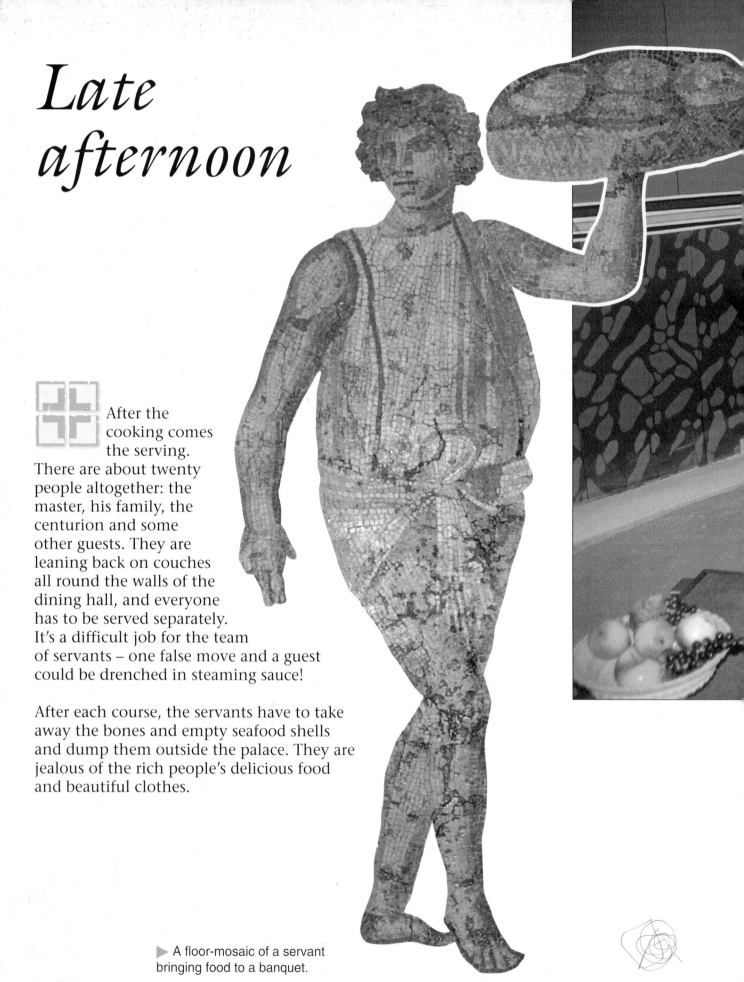

After the cooking comes the serving. There are about twenty people altogether: the master, his family, the centurion and some other guests. They are leaning back on couches all round the walls of the dining hall, and everyone has to be served separately. It's a difficult job for the team of servants – one false move and a guest could be drenched in steaming sauce!

After each course, the servants have to take away the bones and empty seafood shells and dump them outside the palace. They are jealous of the rich people's delicious food and beautiful clothes.

▶ A floor-mosaic of a servant bringing food to a banquet.

▲ A reconstruction of the dining hall at Fishbourne as it might have looked in Roman times.

At least the floor is pleasantly warm for the servants' bare feet. When the guests stop talking and laughing they can hear the hot air roaring through the hypocaust underneath the floor.

► The hypocaust (underfloor heating) at Fishbourne. The floor was raised on pillars of tiles, and the hot air passed through the gaps between the pillars.

Evening

The palace has baths where the family and their wealthy guests can go for a dip. There are three main rooms, one with a pool of hot water, one with a pool of icy cold water and one where the water is pleasantly warm. As they go from pool to pool, some of the people are pink and steaming; others are almost blue with cold. The sudden changes of temperature make them shriek and groan!

The pools aren't big enough for swimming, just for sitting in and talking. If the people want some exercise they can use the sports room next to the baths.

▼ A servant scrapes a metal tool over his master's skin to remove the slightest trace of dirt.

The kitchen is tidy and most of the servants have gone away to their wooden homes, but one has been told to make a new dice from a piece of bone. She won't get very much sleep tonight.

▲ Playing a game with dice, like the men in this mosaic, was a way to relax before bed, as long as no one became too excited and bet all his money!

Places to visit

Fishbourne Roman Palace is near Chichester in West Sussex. If you live in the south of England it is easy to get to because Fishbourne railway station is nearby.

If you live in other parts of Britain you may find it easier to get to other sites and museums where Roman remains can be seen, and the list and map on these pages should help you.

Roman Army Museum, Carvoran, Greenhead, near Carlisle, Cumbria.

Segontium Roman Fort and Museum, Caernarfon, Gwynedd.

Wall Roman Site (Letocetum), Wall, near Lichfield, Staffordshire.

National Museum of Antiquities
of Scotland, Edinburgh.

Arbeia Roman Fort and Museum,
South Shields, Tyne and Wear.

Hadrian's Wall and
Housesteads Fort, Bardon Mill,
Hexham, Northumberland.

Burgh Castle,
near Great Yarmouth,
Norfolk.

British Museum, Great
Russell Street, London.

Museum of London,
London Wall, London.

Corinium Museum,
Cirencester,
Gloustershire.

Chedworth Roman Villa,
Yanworth,
near Cheltenham,
Gloucestershire.

Roman Baths and
Museum, Bath, Avon.

Glossary

archaeologist Someone who studies the past from remains.

audience chamber A room for listening to someone speak.

cargo Goods carried by ship.

centurion A Roman soldier in charge of 80 men.

craftsperson A skilled worker.

emperor The man in charge of the whole Roman empire.

hypocaust The Roman form of central heating.

invade To attack a country with an army.

luxury Something expensive that gives people pleasure.

mortar A sort of cement.

ornamental Decorative.

pillar A stone post.

scribe A person who writes down what is said in meetings.

shrine A building in which the gods are worshipped.

spit A prong on which meat is roasted.

toga a piece of cloth worn by Roman men around their shoulders and body.

Index

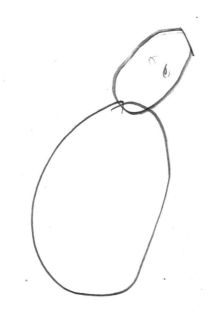

33

34